MW01518022

Presented to HAFIZ SHAHZIR

From HAFIZ ISA'S DAD

Date Jul 17, 2014

MUHAMMAD
THE HERO AS PROPHET

THOMAS CARLYLE

With an introduction by
RUQAIYYAH WARIS MAQSOOD

Goodword
B · O · O · K · S

First published in England in 1841
© Goodword Books 2008
Reprinted 2001, 2002, 2003, 2004, 2005, 2008

Goodword Books
1, Nizamuddin West Market
New Delhi - 110 013
email: info@goodwordbooks.com
Printed in India

www.goodwordbooks.com

INTRODUCTION

Thomas Carlyle (1795-1881), born in Ecclefechan, Dumfriesshire, Scotland, was a historian and essayist, the second son of James Carlyle. James Carlyle was a deeply religious man, with profound Calvinist convictions, whose character and way of life had a lasting influence on his famous son.

(Calvinists are a type of Christian very different to the Roman Catholic. The most obvious features of Roman Catholicism are ritual pomp and ceremony, an influential priesthood of a paternal nature, reverence for the Virgin Mary, and such things as decoration, incense, statues, making the sign of the cross when praying, and genuflecting when facing the altar and at certain times during the prayer. Calvinists are puritanical, with a strong inclination to make religion a matter of personal piety and morality; they have distaste for waste, decoration, self-abasement and the notion that a priest is in any way a superior figure. Each individual is his own 'priest' and stands before God responsible for himself. The leaders in this particular Church are not priests, but ministers. It will immediately be noticed that these ideas lie more easy with the Muslim way, and may explain Carlyle's sympathy towards Islam to a great extent. The Muslims he knew displayed the same Calvinistic qualities, to an even greater and more personally devout degree.)

As a youth, he attended village school in Ecclefechan, followed by a time at Annan Academy where he was very unhappy and suffered from bullying; he then became a student at Edinburgh University. He was a deeply religious man, and his father hoped he would become a minister in the Church, but Thomas became increasingly unsure of this vocation. His aptitude was for mathematics, and he became a teacher of that subject. However, he soon felt uncomfortable with teaching, and in 1819 returned to Edinburgh University to study law. Once again, satisfaction eluded him and he became increasingly depressed and lonely. During this period he was poor, isolated, and conscious of intense spiritual struggles.

In 1821 he experienced a kind of renewed religious conversion, a personal experience of *taqwa*, but rather sadly the dominant feeling that followed was hatred of the devil rather than love of God. At this time he began to study the German language and German philosophy, and translated Goethe's William Meister's Appren-ticeship.

In 1826 he married Jane Welsh, and was known to be a difficult and irritable husband; although they cared for and respected each other, their life together was full of quarrels and misunderstandings. He became a regular contributor to the Edinburgh Review, and wrote *Sartor Resartus*, a strange mix of autobiography and German philosophy. The main theme of this book was that all the old intellectual forms of man's deepest convictions were dead, and it was time to find new ones to fit the times.

In 1834 when he moved to London after failing to gain suitable employment, he entered a period of great financial insecurity. The couple lived on his savings for around a year, while he wrote his ambitious historical work on the French Revolution. Carlyle saw the French Revolution as an inevitable judgement on the folly and selfishness of the monarchy. When the manuscript was finished, he lent it to the philosopher John Stuart Mill, and it was accidentally destroyed in a fire. This was an enormous blow, but Carlyle set to rewriting it, and finished it in 1837. At last he won serious acclaim and popular success, and invitations to lecture. This made him financially secure and in 1840 he published 'Chartism', showing himself to be a bitter opponent of conventional economic theory.

In 1841, his great work *On Heroes, Hero Worship and the Heroic in History* appeared, the work from which the extract published here is taken. In it, he expressed his Calvinistic admiration of strength, particularly when combined with purity, genuineness, and the conviction of a God-given mission.

He discussed the development of

man's attitude to the hero, from the pagan myths which mistakenly worshipped heroes as divinities to those who respected heroes as prophets, poets, men of letters, priests and kings. The poets he chose were Dante and Shakespeare; the priests were Luther and Knox; the men of letters were Johnson and Burns; and the kings were Cromwell and Napoleon. What is most interesting, however, was that of all the prophets he might have chosen, it was Muhammad the Prophet of Islam that he chose for his example of the best of this genre.

Carlyle was never able to respect ordinary men, and he was particularly at odds with the Christian emphasis on emotionalism, tolerating and constantly forgiving the weak and sinful. This he regarded as lacking in backbone. His

Calvinist nature and background gave him the sincere desire to denounce all evil and conquer weakness in one's self.

It was the strength of Muhammad, coupled with his fiery devotion to God and a religion that did not depend on mythology but natural and scientific reason, and a strictly disciplined personal piety and practice that appealed to him.

His essay on the Prophet of Islam, Muhammad (upon whom be peace) is a fascinating insight into the serious thoughts of a man who was in a way on the brink of Islam, and might easily have taken the fateful step into Islam himself had the 'equipment' he was using to study the words of the Qur'an not been so inadequate. Unfortunately, he could not speak Arabic, and made the great mistake of forming a judgement on the

Qur'an from the translations available to him under the assumption that these were sufficient and fair versions.

On going through this extract, Muslim readers will see that whereas he had opinions of the Qur'an which they will find hard to understand, he nevertheless had a deep reverence for Islam, for Muslims in general, and in particular for the Prophet.

Reading his words about the Prophet comes strangely to us now, at the end of the twentieth century, because the Western study of Islam has progressed so much during the past hundred years. Only really ignorant fools would attack Islam these days in the terms that were common in Carlyle's time.

Carlyle was what we might call an Orientalist; that is to say, he had a deep respect and reverence for Islam, but viewed it entirely from a Christian point of view in which he naturally assumed Christianity to be the superior faith. It was apparently unthinkable to him that any Christian could leave that faith to be converted to Islam which accounts for the odd struggle with himself that a person of insight can perceive in his pages about the Prophet.

All the way through, he admits the truths of Islam, the superior faith and disciplines, the high moral calling, the genuine insight, and so forth. Yet he cannot bring himself to take that step taken in recent years by so many Westerners, that of admitting that Islam could actually be in the right, and Christianity to be the faith that is in error.

Many Western people held typical

stereotyped opinions based on absurd generalisations. They held a dim view of the character of 'the typical oriental' holding the credulity, exaggerations, lying and rip-offs encountered by some travellers to be typical of Muslims in general, since Islam was the faith of these folk, who were either innocent of philosophical reality to the point of being ridiculous, or scoundrels. It was also assumed that they were sex-mad, keeping harems of women in subjection to their every whim. These notions were commonplace, but were balanced by another generalisation, the 'noble desert bedouin' a brave, hospitable and much-to-be admired character.

So, when Carlyle discussed the Prophet, and aspects of the faith of Islam, we must always bear in mind that he was giving his honest opinion which was hampered by these various factors.

One will find in this text much to annoy the Muslim reader. Carlyle presented Islam not as the preaching of the Revelation of God, but as the 'rude message' of an illiterate and almost savage individual, albeit a genuine and admirable individual. He assumed that his readers (who were, of course, superior to these 'rude wild men') were 'in no danger of becoming Muhammadans'. The very mention of the word 'Muhammadans' is typical as this is the term Muslims were known by at the time Carlyle wrote.

Bearing all this in mind, what Carlyle did was to forcefully oppose the current 'Christian' presentation of the Prophet as a scheming impostor, a 'Falsehood incarnate', or that his religion was 'a mere mass of quackery and fatuity', with a gross, material and sensual Heaven and Hell, and that it encouraged incest and lascivious behaviour (the harem and facility of divorce) and downgraded the status of women.

It may astound today's Muslims to know that critics of Islam in Carlyle's time had even put about such stupid stories as that the Prophet had trained a pigeon to pick peas out of his ear—and this was supposed to be his devious attempt to portray the angel Gabriel, or the Holy Spirit! Presumably this nonsense was based on the Gospel story of the Holy Spirit descending upon Prophet Jesus at his baptism in the form of a dove. The critics blithely supposed that Muhammad knew a garbled version of this, and deliberately used a pigeon to dupe people. The Prophet was being portrayed as a gross impostor, an Anti-Christ.

It seems incredible to serious-minded Muslims that Westerners could have considered such nonsense to be true for one moment. Carlyle's defence of the Prophet is therefore all the more interesting and brave, because despite all the handicaps of his inadequate knowledge and the vehement opposition to Islam of his time, he could see in the Prophet and his message nothing but good.

The qualities of a bold Calvinist, who cared nothing for the opinions of men but only for the truth and honourable pious living, were exactly what was required to take on the stupid and fatuous criticisms of ignorant non-Muslims. Carlyle was totally convinced, without doubt, that the Prophet was a genuine man, without the slightest shred of personal ambition of duplicity. 'A false man found a religion? Why, a false man cannot build a brick house!' His house certainly would not stand for twelve centuries—it would flounder and fall straight away.

Carlyle presented what he knew of the life of the Prophet in a very positive way. To this day, it stands a very clear, concise, knowledgeable and fair account. His description of the Prophet's physical person, and his life and relationship with Khadijah are touchingly outlined. As for the Prophet's faith, and its success, he pointed out that nothing can conquer that which is better than itself—the truth will show up at last; as the Qur'an says, 'Truth stands out clear from error'.

However, Carlyle still regarded Islam as a 'confused form of Christianity', and assumed that the Prophet gained his 'imperfect knowledge' of Biblical stories and characters not from direct Revelation (which happened to present the lessons of the Bible heroes differently from the Bible version) but from his contact with Jews and Christian peoples. He then assumed that the prophet had not got enough education or knowledge to present these stories except imperfectly. He particularly drew attention to the story that when the Prophet was around 14 years of age, he and his uncle Abu Talib used to reside on their travels with a Nestorian Christian monk, Sergius (but he does not give the source of this interesting suggestion).

Carlyle also assumed, like most Christian thinkers, that Christianity was promoted nobly and peacably, converting people by gentle missionary work, as opposed to Muslims converting people by frightening them with the sword. In the Crusades, the knights were perfect Christian gentlemen of honour and the Muslims were the infidel, exactly the opposite way round from how Muslims see it! Yet Carlyle could see that no one would have followed the sword of Muhammad had they not been totally convinced of the truths of his teaching. Ali was commended as being 'worthy of a Christian knighthood'.

For Carlyle, the Prophet was a genuine man of insight, a great leader, a devout and humble man, yet the truth of his religion was 'embedded in a portentous error and falsehood'. This was because, to him, Christianity was the truth and the only way to Heaven. One finds Carlyle calling Islam 'a bastard kind of Christianity but a living kind'; and again, 'a confused form of Christianity'. It should be made clear that this was not intended by Carlyle as an insult, but as praise; indeed Carlyle gave Islam the highest accolade when he went so far as to state that Islam was 'properly the soul of Christianity'.

This is precisely what today's Christian converts to Islam feel. They do not feel traitors to Christianity, or that they have in any way reduced the person of Jesus by exchanging their view that he was the Son of God in a Trinity for the view that he was one of God's greatest chosen messengers. They feel that Islam teaches what Christianity should be teaching; and when they study their Gospels, with Muslim insight they can see that Islam is what Jesus actually taught.

Carlyle said: 'Muhammad's creed we call a kind of Christianity... a better kind than that of those miserable Syrian sects with their vain janglings!' What a pity he did not take the great step of courage of his own convictions, and come across Islam himself.

The sad fact was that he did not enjoy reading the version of the Qur'an that was available to him, and could not make a lot of it. Sale's translation he calls 'as toilsome reading as I ever undertook'; a wearisome, confused jumble, crude, incondite; endless iterations, long-windedness, entanglement... insupportable stupidity, in short nothing but a sense of duty could carry a European through the Qur'an.

He felt he had to plough through unreadable masses of lumber to get glimpses of the remarkable man who had written it, another orientalist mistaken assumption. No non-Muslim ever assumes that the Qur'an is precisely what it purports to be—direct revelation from the One True God.

He claimed the Qur'an was 'written, as far as writing goes, as badly as almost any book ever written. One feels it difficult to see how any mortal could ever consider the Qur'an as a book written in Heaven.' He dismisses the hostile notion of such writers as Prideaux that chapter after chapter of the Qur'an was simply got up to excuse and varnish the author's (the Prophet's) successive sins, or forward his ambitions. Carlyle does not doubt the Prophet's sincerity for one moment. But he saw the Qur'an as the confused utterings of a 'great rude human soul in ferment', earnest, struggling vehemently to 'utter himself in words', with his thoughts in a 'chaotic, inarticulate state'.

Having said all this, all of which is highly offensive to Muslims, and all of which was Carlyle's genuine opinion, he sees the Prophet as one of the world's greatest heroes, and presents him as such. It is notable that he does not mention any single supposed sin or imperfection in the Prophet's life or character, and points out very clearly that the Prophet did not initiate practices the West found so abhorrent (like polygamy), but only imposed limits on what was already the current practice.

In case noble Muslim readers of the Qur'an, who are entirely devoted to its words, feel that Carlyle must have been quite mad, let me state my own personal experience that when I first read it, in a poor translation, I tended to react in rather the same way as Carlyle. In my opinion, the best translation Westerners have to date is that of the Muhammad Asad, printed in Gibraltar. Before his version, the Qur'an had never been presented in any European language in a manner which would make it truly comprehensible.

(Muhammad Asad was born Leopold Weiss, in Poland, of Jewish parents. He became the confidant of many major

Muslim figures, including King Abdul Aziz Ibn Saud and his son King Faisal. He died in 1992).

In 1865 Carlyle was offered the rectorship of Edinburgh University, where he became a byword for high moral exhortation.

Suddenly, his wife, Jane, died and Carlyle never completely recovered from this blow. He lived another 15 years, weary, bored and a partial recluse, writing other famous works—*The Early Kings of Norway, An Essay on the Portraits of John Knox* (1875) and *Reminiscences* in 1881. He edited his wife's letters and published them in 1883.

When he died, Westminster Abbey was offered for his burial, but he was buried, according to his own wish, beside his parents at Ecclefechan.

If only Carlyle had had access to an adequate translation of the Qur'an with scholarly footnotes, then his opinions would have been completely different, and he might well have taken that step so well-known to 'reverts' to Islam from Christianity, of realising that they had indeed found the truth, and the Straight Path to Allah.

Ruqaiyyah Waris Maqsood
Hull (U.K.)
January 29, 1997

MUHAMMAD

THE HERO AS PROPHET

From the first rude times of paganism among the Scandinavians in the North, we advance to a very different epoch of religion, among a very different people: Muhammadanism among the Arabs. A great change; what a change and progress is indicated here, in the universal condition and thoughts of men!

The Hero is not now regarded as a God among his fellow men; but as one God-inspired, as a Prophet. It is the second phasis of Hero-worship: the first or oldest, we may say, has passed away without return; in the history of the world there will not again be any man, never so great, whom his fellow men will take for a god. We might rationally ask, did any set of human beings ever really think the man they saw there standing beside them was a god, the maker of this world? Perhaps not: it was usually some man they remembered, or had seen. But neither can this any more be. The Great Man is not recognised henceforth as a god any more.

It was a rude gross error, that of counting the Great Man a god. Yet let us say that it is at all times difficult to know what he is, or how to account for him and receive him! The most significant feature in the history of an epoch is the manner it has of welcoming a Great Man. Ever, to the true instincts of men, there is something godlike in him. Whether they shall take him to be a god, to be a prophet, or what they shall take him to be? that is ever a grand question; by their way of answering that, we shall see, as through a little window, into the very heart of these men's spiritual condition. For at bottom the Great Man, as he comes from the hand of Nature, is ever the same kind of thing; Odin, Luther, Johnson, Burns; I hope to make it appear that these are all originally of one stuff; that only by the world's reception of them, and the shapes they assume, are they so immeasurably diverse. The worship of

Odin astonishes us, to fall prostrate before the Great Man, into deliquium of love and wonder over him, and feel in their hearts that he was a denizen of the skies, a god! This was imperfect enough: but to welcome, for example, a Burns as we did, was that what we can call perfect? The most precious gift that Heaven can give to the Earth; a man of 'genius' as we call it; the Soul of a Man actually sent down from the skies with a God's-message to us, this we waste away as an idle artificial firework, sent to amuse us a little, and sink it into ashes, wreck and ineffectuality: such reception of a Great Man I do not call very perfect either! Looking into the heart of the thing, one may perhaps call that of Burns a still uglier phenomenon, betokening still sadder imperfections in mankind's ways, than the Scandinavian method itself! To fall into mere unreasoning deliquium of love and admiration, was not good; but such unreasoning, even supercilious no-love at all is perhaps still worse! It is a thing forever changing, this of Hero-worship: different in each age, difficult to do well in any age. Indeed, the heart of the whole business of the age, one may say, is to do it well.

We have chosen Muhammad not as the most eminent Prophet; but as the one we are free to speak of. He is by no means the truest of Prophets; but I do esteem him a true one. Further, as there is no danger of our becoming, any of us, Muhammadans, I mean to say all the good of him I justly can. It is the way to get at his secret: let us try to understand what he meant with the world; what the world meant and means with him, will then be a more answerable question. Our current hypothesis about Muhammad, that he was a scheming Impostor, a Falsehood incarnate, that his religion is a mere mass of quackery and fatuity, begins really to be now untenable to any one. The lies, which well-meaning zeal has heaped round this man, are disgraceful to ourselves only. When Pococke inquired of Grotius, where the proof was of that story of the pigeon, trained to pick peas from Muhammad's ear, and pass for an angel dictating to him? Grotius answered that there was no proof! It is really time to dismiss all that. The word this man spoke has been the life-guidance now of a hundred-and-eighty millions of men these twelve-hundred years. These hundred-and-eighty millions were made by God as well as we. A greater number of God's creatures believe in Muhammad's word at this hour than in any other word whatever. Are we to suppose that it was a miserable piece of spiritual legerdemain, this which so many creatures of the Almighty have lived by and died by? I, for my part, cannot form any such supposition. I will believe most things sooner than that. One would be entirely at a loss what to think of this world at all, if quackery so grew and were sanctioned here.

Alas, such theories are very lamentable. If we would attain to knowledge of anything in God's true Creation, let us disbelieve them wholly! They are the product of an Age of Scepticism; they indicate the saddest spiritual paralysis, and mere death-life of the souls of men: more godless theory, I think, was never promulgated in this earth. A false man found a religion? Why, a false man cannot build a brick house! If he do not know and follow truly the properties of mortar, burnt clay and what else he works in, it is no house that he makes, but a rubbish-heap. It will not stand for twelve centuries, to lodge a hundred-and-eighty millions; it will fall straightway. A man must conform himself to Nature's laws, be verily in communion with Nature and the truth of things, or Nature will answer him, No, not at all! Speciosities are specious, ah me! A Cagliostro, many Cagliostros, prominent world leaders, do prosper by their quackery, for a day. It is like a forged bank note; they get it passed out of their worthless hands: others, not they, have to smart for it. Nature bursts up in fire-flames, French Revolutions and such-like, proclaiming with terrible veracity that forged notes are forged.

But of a Great Man especially, of him I will venture to assert that it is incredible he should have been other than true. It seems to me the primary foundation of him, and of all that can lie in him, this. No Mirabeau, Napoleon, Burns, Cromwell, no man adequate to do anything, but is first of all in right earnest about it; what I call a sincere man. I should say sincerity, a deep, great, genuine sincerity, is the first characteristic of all men in any way heroic. Not the sincerity that calls itself sincere; ah no, that is a very poor matter indeed; a shallow braggart conscious sincerity; oftenest self-conceit mainly. The Great

Man's sincerity is of the kind he cannot speak of in sincerity; for what a man can talk accurately by the law of truth for one day? No, the Great Man does not boast himself sincere, far from that; perhaps does not ask himself if he is so: I would say rather, his sincerity does not depend on himself; he cannot help being sincere! The great Fact of Existence is great to him. Fly as he will, he cannot get out of the awful presence of this Reality. His mind is so made; he is great by that, first of all. Fearful and wonderful, real as Life, real as Death, is this Universe to him. Though all men should forget its truth, and walk in a vain show, he cannot. At all moments the Flame-image glares in upon him; undeniable, there, there! I wish you to take this as my primary definition of a Great Man. A little man may have this, it is competent to all men that God has made: but a Great Man cannot be without it.

Such a man is what we call an original man; he comes to us at first-hand. A messenger he, sent from the Infinite Unknown with tidings to us. We may call him Poet, Prophet, God; in one way or other, we all feel that the words he utters are as no other man's words. Direct from the Inner Fact of things; he lives, and has to live, in daily communion with that. Hearsays cannot hide it from him; he is blind, homeless, miserable, following hearsays; it glares in upon him. Really, his utterances, are they not a kind of 'revelation;' what we must call such for want of some other name? It is from the heart of the world that he comes; he is portion of the primal reality of things.

God has made many revelations: but this man, too, has not God made him, the latest and newest of all? The 'inspiration of the Almighty gave him understanding:' we must listen before all to him.

This Muhammad, then, we will in no wise consider as an Inanity and Theatricality, a poor conscious ambitious schemer; we cannot conceive him so. The rude message he delivered was a real one withal; an earnest confused voice from the unknown Deep. The man's words were not false, nor his workings here below; no Inanity and Simulacrum; a fiery mass of Life cast up from the great bosom of Nature herself. To kindle the world; the world's Maker had ordered it so. Neither can the faults, imperfections, insincerities even, of Muhammad, if such were never so well proved against him, shake this primary fact about him.

On the whole, we make too much of faults; the details of the business hide the real centre of it. Faults? The greatest of faults, I should say, is to be conscious of none. Readers of the Bible above all, one would think, might know better. Who is called there 'the man according to God's own heart?' David, the Hebrew King, had fallen into sins enough; blackest crimes; there was no want of sins. And thereupon the unbelievers sneer and ask: Is this your man according to God's heart? The sneer, I must say, seems to me but a shallow one. What are faults, what are the outward details of a life; if the inner secret of it, the remorse, temptations, true, often-baffled, never-ended struggle of it, be forgotten? 'It is not in man that walks to direct his steps.'

The deadliest sin, I say, were that same supercilious consciousness of no sin; that is death; the heart so conscious is divorced from sincerity, humility and fact; is dead: it is 'pure' as dead dry sand is pure. David's life and history, as written for us in those Psalms of his, I consider to be the truest emblem ever given of a man's moral progress and warfare here below. All earnest souls will ever discern in it the faithful struggle of an earnest human soul towards what is good and best. Struggle often baffled, sore baffled, down as into entire wreck; yet a struggle never ended; even, with tears, repentance, true unconquerable purpose, begun anew. Poor human nature! Is not a man's walking, in truth, always that: 'a succession of falls'? Man can do no other. In this wild element of a Life, he has to struggle onwards; now fallen, deep-abased; and ever, with tears, repentance, with bleeding heart, he has to rise again, struggle again still onwards. That his struggle be a faithful unconquerable one: that is the question of questions. We will put up with many sad details, if the soul of it were true. Details by themselves will never teach us what it is. I believe we mis-estimate Muhammad's faults even as faults: but the secret of him will never be got by dwelling there. We will leave all this behind us; and assuring ourselves that he did mean some true thing, ask candidly what it was or might be.

These Arabs, Muhammad was born among are certainly a notable people. Their country itself is notable; the fit habitation for such a race. Savage, inaccessible rock-mountains, great grim deserts, alternating with beautiful strips of verdure: wherever water is, there is greenness, beauty; odoriferous balm-shrubs, date-trees, frankincense-trees. Consider that wide waste horizon of sand, empty, silent, like a sand-sea, dividing habitable place from habitable. You are all alone there, left alone with the Universe; by day a fierce sun blazing down on it with intolerable radiance; by night the great deep Heaven with its stars. Such a country is fit for a swift-handed, deep-hearted race of men. There is something most agile, active, and yet most meditative, enthusiastic in the Arab character. The Persians are called the French of the East; we will call the Arabs Oriental Italians. A gifted noble people; a people of wild strong feelings, and of iron restraint over these: the characteristic of noble-mindedness, of genius. The wild Bedouin welcomes the stranger to his tent, as one having right to all that is there; were it his worst enemy, he will slay his foal to treat him, will serve him with sacred hospitality for three days, will set him fairly on his way; and then, by another law as sacred, kill him if he can. In words too, as in action. They are not a loquacious people, taciturn rather; but eloquent, gifted when they do speak. An earnest, truthful kind of men. They are, as we know, of Jewish kindred: but with that deadly terrible earnestness of the Jews they seem to combine something graceful, brilliant, which is not Jewish. They had 'Poetic contests' among them before the time of Muhammad. Sale says, at Ocadh, (Ukaz) in the South of Arabia, there were yearly fairs, and there, when the merchandising was done, poets sang for prizes: the wild people gathered to hear that.

One Jewish quality these Arabs manifest; the outcome of many or of all high qualities: what we may call religiosity. From the old they had been zealous worshippers, according to their light. They worshipped the stars, as Sabeans; worshipped many natural objects, recognised them as symbols, immediate manifestations, of the Maker of Nature. It was wrong; and yet not wholly wrong. All God's works are still in a sense symbols of God. Do we not, as I urged, still account it a merit to recognise a certain inexhaustible significance, 'poetic beauty' as we name it, in all natural objects whatsoever? A man is a poet, and honoured, for being that, and speaking or singing it, a kind of diluted worship. They had many Prophets, these Arabs; Teachers each to his tribe, each according to the light he had. But indeed, have we not from of old the noblest of proofs, still palpable to every one of us, of what devoutness and noble-mindedness had dwelt in these rustic thoughtful peoples? Biblical critics seem agreed that our own Book of Job was written in this region of the world. I call that apart from all theories about it, one of the grandest things ever written with pen. One feels, indeed, as if it were not Hebrew; such a noble universality, different from noble patriotism or sectarianism, reigns in it. A noble Book; all men's Book! It is our first, oldest statement of the never-ending Problem, man's destiny, and God's ways with him here in this earth. And all in such free flowing outlines; grand in its sincerity, in its simplicity; in its epic melody, and repose of reconcilement. There is the seeing eye, the mildly understanding heart. So true every way; true eyesight and vision for all things; material things no less than spiritual: the Horse, 'hast thou clothed his neck with thunder?' he 'laughs at the shaking of the spear!' Such living likenesses were never since drawn. Sublime sorrow, sublime reconciliation; oldest choral melody as of the heart of mankind; so soft, and great; as the summer midnight, as the world with its seas and stars! There is nothing written, I think, in the Bible or out of it, of equal literary merit.

To the idolatrous Arabs one of the

most ancient universal objects of worship was that Black Stone, still kept in the building called Ka'bah at Makkah. Diodorus Siculus mentions this Ka'bah in a way not to be mistaken, as the oldest, most honoured temple in his time; that is, some half-century before our Era. Silvestre de Sacy says there is some likelihood that the Black Stone is an aerolite. In that case, some man might see it fall out of Heaven! It stands now beside the Well Zamzam; the Ka'bah is built over both. A Well is in all places a beautiful affecting object, gushing out like life from the hard earth; still more so in those hot dry countries, where it is the first condition of being. The Well Zamzam has its name from the bubbling sound of the waters, zam-zam; they think it is the Well which Hagar found with her little

Ishmael in the wilderness; the aerolite and it have been sacred now, and had a Ka'bah over them, for thousands of years. A curious object that Ka'bah! There it stands at this hour, in the black cloth-covering the Sultan sends it yearly; 'twenty-seven cubits high;' with circuit, with double circuit of pillars, with festoon-rows of lamps and quaint ornaments: the lamps will be lighted again this night, to glitter again under the stars. An authentic fragment of the oldest Past. It is the *Qiblah* of all Muslim: from Delhi all onwards to Morocco, the eyes of innumerable praying men are turned towards it, five times, this day and all days: one of the notablest centres in the Habitation of Men.

It had been from the sacredness attached to this Ka'bah Stone and Hagar's

Well, from the pilgrimings of all tribes of Arabs thither, that Makkah took its rise as a Town. A great town once, though much decayed now. It has no natural advantage for a town; stands in a sandy hollow amid bare barren hills, at a distance from the sea; its provisions, its very bread, have to be imported. But so many pilgrims needed lodgings: and then all places of pilgrimage do, from the first, become places of trade. The first day pilgrims meet, merchants have also met; where men see themselves assembled for one object, they find that they can accomplish other objects which depend on meeting together. Makkah became the Fair of all Arabia. And thereby indeed the chief staple and warehouse of whatever Commerce there was between the Indian and the Western countries,

Syria, Egypt, even Italy. It had at one time a population of 100,000; buyers, forwarders of those Eastern and Western products; importers for their own behoof of provisions and corn. The government was a kind of irregular aristocratic republic, not without a touch of theocracy. Ten Men of a chief tribe, chosen in some rough way, were Governors of Makkah and Keepers of the Ka'bah. The Quraysh were the chief tribe in Muhammad's time; his own family was of that tribe. The rest of the Nation, fractioned and cut asunder by deserts, lived under similar rude patriarchal governments by one or several: herdsmen, carriers, traders, generally robbers too; being often at war one with another, or with all: held together by no open bond, if it were not this meeting at the Ka'bah, where all forms of Arab Idolatry assembled in common adoration; held mainly by the inward indissoluble bond of a common blood and language. In this way had the Arabs lived for long ages, unnoticed by the world; a people of great qualities, unconsciously waiting for the day when they should become notable to all the world. Their Idolatries appear to have been in a tottering state; much was getting into confusion and fermentation among them.Obscure tidings of the most important Event ever transacted in this world, the Life and Death of the Divine Man in Judea, at once the symptom and cause of immeasurable change to all people in the world, had in the course of centuries reached into Arabia too; and could not but, of itself, have produced fermentation there.

It was among this Arab people, so circumstanced, in the year 570 of our Era, that the man Muhammad was born. He was of the family of Hashim, of the Quraysh tribe as we said; though poor, connected with the chief persons of his country. Almost at his birth he lost his Father; at the age of six years his Mother, too, a woman noted for her beauty, her worth and sense: he fell to the charge of his Grandfather, an old man, a hundred years old. A good old man: Muhammad's Father 'Abdullah, had been his youngest favourite son. He saw in Muhammad, with old life-worn eyes, a century old, the lost 'Abdullah come back again, all that was left of 'Abdullah. He loved the little orphan Boy greatly; used to say, They must take care of that beautiful little Boy, nothing in their kindred was more precious than he. At his death, while the boy was still but two years old, he left him in charge of Abu Talib, the eldest of the Uncles, as to him that now was head of the house. By this Uncle, a just and rational man as everything betokens, Muhammad was brought up in the best Arab way.

Muhammad, as he grew up, accompanied his Uncle on trading journeys and suchlike; in his eighteenth year one finds him a fighter following his Uncle in war. But perhaps the most significant of all his journeys is one we find noted as of some years' earlier date: a journey to the Fairs of Syria. The young man here first came in contact with a quite foreign world, with one foreign element of endless moment to him: the

Christian Religion. I know not what to make of that 'Sergius, the Nestorian Monk,' whom Abu Talib and he are said to have lodged with; or how much any monk could have taught one still so young. Probably enough it is greatly exaggerated, this of the Nestorian Monk. Muhammad was only fourteen; had no language but his own; much in Syria must have been a strange unintelligible whirlpool to him. But the eyes of the lad were open; glimpses of many things would doubtless be taken in, and lie very enigmatic as yet, which were to ripen in a strange way into views, into beliefs and insights one day. The journeys to Syria were probably the beginning of much to Muhammad.

One other circumstance we must not forget: that he had no school-learning; of the thing we call school-learning none at all. The art of writing was but just introduced into Arabia; it seems to be the true opinion that Muhammad never could write! Life in the Desert, with its experiences, was all his education. What of this infinite Universe he, from his dim place, with his own eyes and thoughts, could take in, so much and no more of it was he to know. Curious, if we will reflect on it, this of having no books Except by what he could see for himself, or hear of by uncertain rumour of speech in the obscure Arabian Desert, he could know nothing. The wisdom that had been before him or at a distance from him in the world, was in a manner as good as not there for him. Of the great brother souls, flame-beacons through so many lands and times, no one directly communicates with this great soul. He is alone there, deep down in the bosom of the Wilderness; has to grow up so, alone with Nature and his own Thoughts.

But, from an early age, he had been remarked as a thoughtful man. His companions named him 'Al Amin, The Faithful.' A man of truth and fidelity; true in what he did, in what he spoke and thought. They noted that he always meant something. A man rather taciturn in speech; silent when there was nothing to be said; but pertinent, wise, sincere, when he did speak; always throwing light on the matter. This is the only sort of speech worth speaking! Through life we find him to have been regarded as an altogether solid, brotherly, genuine man. A serious, sincere character; yet amiable, cordial, companionable, jocose even; a good laugh in him withal: there are men whose laugh is as untrue as anything about them; who cannot laugh. One hears of Muhammad's beauty: his fine sagacious honest face, brown florid complexion, beaming black eyes; I somehow like too that vein on the brow, which swelled-up black when he was in anger: like the 'horse-shoe vein' in Scott's Redgauntlet. It was a kind of feature in the Hashim family, this black swelling vein the brow; Muhammad had it prominent, as would appear. A spontaneous, passionate, yet just, true-meaning man! Full of wild faculty, fire and light; of wild worth, all uncultured; working out his life-task in the depths of the Deserts there.

How he was placed with Khadijah, a rich Widow, as her Steward, and travelled in her business, again to the Fairs of Syria; how he managed all, as one can well understand, with fidelity, adroitness; how her gratitude, her regard for him grew: the story of their marriage is altogether a graceful intelligible one, as told us by the Arab authors. He was twenty-five; she forty, though still beautiful. He seems to have lived in a most affectionate, peaceable, wholesome way with this wedded benefactress; loving her truly, and her alone. It goes greatly against the impostor theory, the fact that he lived in this entirely unexceptionable, entirely quiet and commonplace way, till the heat of his years was done. He was forty before he talked of any mission from Heaven. All his irregularities, real and supposed, date from after his fiftieth year, when the good Khadijah died. All his 'ambition,' seemingly, had been, hitherto, to live an honest life; his 'fame,' the more good opinion of neighbours that knew him, had been sufficient hitherto. Not till he was already getting old, the prurient heat of his life all burnt out, and peace growing to be the chief thing this world could give him, did he start on the 'career of ambition;' and, belying all his past character and existence, set up as a wretched empty charlatan to acquire what he could now no longer enjoy! For my share, I have no faith whatever in that.

Ah no; this deep-hearted Son of the Wilderness, with his beaming black eyes and open social deep soul, had other thoughts in him than ambition. A silent great soul; he was one of those who cannot but be an earnest; whom Nature herself has appointed to be sincere. While others walk in formulas and hearsays, contented enough to dwell there, this man could not screen himself in formulas; he was alone with his own soul and the reality of things. The great Mystery of Existence, as I said, glared in upon him, with its terrors, with its splendours; no hearsays could hide that unspeakable fact, "Here am I!" Such sincerity, as we named it, has in very truth something of divine. The word of such a man is a Voice direct from Nature's own Heart. Men do and must listen to that as to nothing else; all else is wind in comparison. From of old, a thousand thoughts, in his pilgrimings and wanderings, had been in this man: What am I? What is this unfathomable Thing I live in, which men name Universe? What is Life; what is Death? What am I to believe? What am I to do? The grim rocks of Mount Hira, of Mount Sinai, and stern sandy solitudes answered not. The great Heaven rolling silent overhead, with its blue-glancing stars, answered not. There was no answer. The man's own soul, and what of God's inspiration dwelt there, had to answer!

It is the thing which all men have to ask themselves; which we, too, have to ask, and answer. This wild man felt it to be of infinite moment; all other things of no moment whatever in comparison. The jargon of argumentative Greek Sects, vague traditions of Jews, the stupid routine of Arab Idolatry; there was no answer in these. A Hero, as I repeat, has this first distinction, which indeed we may call first and last, the Alpha and

Omega of his whole Heroism. That he looks through the shows of things into things. Use and wont, respectable hearsay, respectable formula; all these are good, or are not good. There is something behind and beyond all these, which all these must correspond with, be the image of, or they are Idolatries; 'bits of black wood pretending to be God;' to the earnest soul a mockery and abomination. Idolatries never so gilded, waited on by heads of the Quraysh, will do nothing for this man. Though all men walk by them, what good is it? The great Reality stands glaring there upon him. He there has to answer it, or perish miserably. Now, even now, or else through all Eternity never! Answer it; you must find an answer, Ambition? What could all Arabia do for this man; all crowns in the Earth; what could they all do for him? It was not of the Earth he wanted to hear tell; it was of the Heaven above and of the Hell beneath. All crowns and sovereignties whatsoever, where would they in a few brief years be? To be Shaikh of Makkah or Arabia, and have a bit of gilt wood put into your hand, will that be one's salvation? I decidedly think, not. We will leave it altogether, this impostor hypothesis, as not credible; not very tolerable even, worthy chiefly of dismissal by us.

Muhammad had been wont to retire yearly, during the month of Ramadan, into solitude and silence; as indeed was the Arab custom; a praiseworthy custom, which such a man, above all, would find natural and useful. Communing with his own heart, in the silence of the mountains;

himself silent; open to the 'small still voices:' it was a right natural custom! Muhammad was in his fortieth year, when having withdrawn to a cavern in Mount Hira, near Makkah, during this Ramadan to pass the month in prayer, and meditation on those great questions, he one day told his wife Khadijah, who with his household was with him or near him this year, That by the unspeakable special favour of Heaven he had now found it all out; was in doubt and darkness no longer, but saw it all. That all these Idols and Formulas were nothing, miserable bits of wood; that there was One God in and over all; and we must leave all Idols, and look to Him. That God is great; and that there is nothing else great! He is the Reality. Wooden Idols are not real; He is real. He made at first, sustains us yet; we and all things are but the shadow of Him: a transitory garment veiling the Eternal Splendour. 'Allahu akbar, God is great;' and then also 'Islam,' That we must submit to God. That our whole strength lies in resigned submission to Him, whatsoever He do to us. For this world, and for the other! The thing He sends to us, were it death and worse than death, shall be good, shall be best; we resign ourselves to God. 'If Yes, all of us that have any moral life; we all live so. It has ever been held the highest wisdom for a man not merely to submit to Necessity. Necessity will make him submit, but to know and believe well that the stern thing which Necessity had ordered was the wisest, the best, the thing wanted there. To cease his frantic pretension of scanning this great God's World in his small fraction of a brain; to know that it had verily, though deep beyond his soundings, a Just Law, that the soul of it was Good; that his part in it was to conform to the Law of the Whole, and in devout silence follow that; not questioning it obeying it as unquestionable.

I say, this is yet the only true morality known. A man is right and invincible, virtuous and on the road towards sure conquest, precisely while he joins himself to the great deep Law of the World, in spite of all superficial laws, temporary appearances, profit-and-loss calculations; he is victorious while he cooperates with that great central Law, not victorious otherwise: and surely his first chance of cooperating with it, or getting into the course of it, is to know with his whole soul that it is; that it is good, and alone good! This is the soul of Islam; it is properly the soul of Christianity for Islam is definable as a confused form of Christianity; had Christianity not been, neither had it been. Christianity also commands us, before all, to be resigned to God. We are to take no counsel with flesh-and-blood; give ear to no vain cavils, vain sorrows and wishes: to know that we know nothing; that the worst and cruelest to our eyes is not what it seems; that we have to receive whatsoever befalls us as sent from God above, and say, It is good and wise, God is great! "Though He slay me, yet will I trust in Him." Islam means in its way Denial of Self, Annihilation of Self. This is yet the highest Wisdom that Heaven has revealed to our Earth.

Such light had come, as it could, to illuminate the darkness of this wild Arab soul. A confused dazzling splendour as of life and Heaven, in the great darkness which threatened to be death: he called it revelation and the angel Gabriel; who of us yet can know what to call it? It is the 'inspiration of the Almighty that giveth us understanding. To know; to get into the truth of anything, is ever a mystic act, of which the best Logics can but babble on the surface. 'Is not Belief true god-announcing Miracle?' says Novalis. That Muhammad's whole soul, set in flame with this grand Truth vouchsafed him, should feel as if it were important and the only important thing, was very natural. That Providence had unspeakably honoured him by revealing it, saving him from death and darkness;

that he therefore was bound to make known the same to all creatures: this is what was meant by 'Muhammad is the Prophet of God;' this, too, is not without its true meaning.

The good Khadijah, we can fancy, listened to him with wonder, with doubt: at length she answered: Yes, it was true this that he said. One can fancy, too, the boundless gratitude of Muhammad; and how of all the kindnesses she had done him, this of believing the earnest struggling word he now spoke was the greatest. 'It is certain,' says Novalis, 'my Conviction gains infinitely, the moment another soul will believe in it.' It is a boundless favour. He never forgot this good from Khadijah. Long afterwards, 'A'ishah his young favourite wife, a woman who indeed distinguished herself among the Muslims, by all manner of qualities, through her whole long life; this young brilliant 'A'ishah was, one day, questioning him: "Now am not I better than Khadijah? She was a widow; old, and had lost her looks: you love me better than you did her?" "No, by Allah!" answered Muhammad: "No, by Allah! She believed in me when none else would believe. In the whole world I had but one friend, and she was that!" Zayd, his slave, also believed in him; these with his young cousin 'Ali, Abu Talib's son, were his first converts.

He spoke of his Doctrine to this man and that; but most treated it with ridicule, with indifference; in three years, I think, he had gained but thirteen followers. His progress was slow enough. His encouragement to go on was altogether the usual encouragement that such a man in such a case meets: After some three years of small success, he invited forty of his chief kindred to an entertainment; and there stood-up and told them what his pretension was: that he had this thing to promulgate abroad to all men; that it was the highest thing, the one thing; which of them would second him in that? Amid the doubt and silence of all, young 'Ali, as yet a lad of sixteen, impatient of the silence, stood-up, and exclaimed in passionate fierce language, that he would! The assembly, among whom was Abu Talib, Ali's father, could not be unfriendly to Muhammad; yet the sight there, of one unlettered elderly man, with a lad of sixteen, deciding on such an enterprise against all mankind, appeared ridiculous to them;

the assembly broke-up in laughter. Nevertheless it proved not a laughable thing; it was a very serious thing! As for this young 'Ali, one cannot but like him. A noble-minded creature, as he shows himself, now and always afterwards; full of affection, of fiery daring. Something chivalrous in him; brave as a lion; yet with a grace, a truth and affection worthy of Christian knighthood. He died by assassination in the Mosque at Baghdad; a death occasioned by his own generous fairness, confidence in the fairness of others: he said, if the wound proved not unto death, they must pardon the Assassin; but if it did, then they must slay him straightway, that so they two in the same hour might appear before God, and see which side of that quarrel was the just one!

Muhammad naturally gave offence to the Quraysh, Keepers of ·the Ka'bah, superintendents of the Idols. One or two men of influence had joined him: the thing spread slowly, but it was spreading. Naturally he gave offence to everybody: Who is this that pretends to be wiser than we all; that rebukes us all, as mere fools and worshippers of wood! Abu Talib the good Uncle spoke with him: Could he not be silent about all that; believe it all for himself, and not trouble others, anger the chief men, endanger himself and them all, talking of it? Muhammad answered: If the Sun stood on his right hand and the Moon on his left, ordering him to hold his peace, he could not obey! No: there was something in this Truth he had got which was of Nature herself; equal in rank to Sun, or Moon, or whatsoever thing Nature had made. It would speak itself there, so long as the Almighty allowed it, in spite of Sun and Moon, and all Quraysh and all men and things. It must do that, and could do no other. Muḥammad answered so and, they say, 'burst into tears.' Burst into tears: he felt that Abu Talib was good to him; that the task he had got was no soft, but a stern and great one.

He went on speaking to who would listen to him; publishing his Doctrine among the pilgrims as they came to Makkah; gaining adherents in this place and that. Continual contradiction, hatred, open or secret danger attended him. His powerful relations protected Muhammad himself; but by and by, on his own advice, all his adherents had to quit Makkah, and seek refuge in Abyssinia over the sea. The Quraysh grew ever angrier; laid plots, and swore oaths among them, to put Muhammad to death with their own hands. Abu Talib was dead, the good Khadijah was dead. Muhammad is not solicitous of sympathy from us; but his outlook at this time was one of the dismalest. He had to hide in caverns, escape in disguise; fly hither and thither; homeless, in continual peril of his life. More than once it seemed all-over with him; more than once it turned on a straw, some rider's horse taking fright or the like, whether Muhammad and his Doctrine had not ended there, and not been heard of at all. But it was not to end so.

In the thirteenth year of his mission, finding his enemies all banded against him, forty sworn men, one out of every tribe, waiting to take his life, and no continuance possible at Makkah for him any longer, Muhammad fled to the place then called Yathrib, where he had gained some adherents; the place they now call Madinah, or 'Madinat al-Nabi, the City of the Prophet,' from that circumstance. It lay some 200 miles off, through rocks and deserts; not without great difficulty, in such mood as we may fancy, he escaped thither, and found welcome. The whole East dates its era from this Flight, Hijrah as they name it: the Year 1 of this Hijrah is 622 of our Era, the fifty-third of Muhammad's life. He was now becoming an old man; his friends sinking round him one by one; his path desolate, encompassed with danger: unless he could find hope in his own heart, the outward face of things was but hopeless for him. It is so with all men in the like case. Hitherto Muhammad had professed to publish his Religion by the way of preaching and persuasion alone. But now, driven foully out of his native country, since unjust men had not only given no ear to his earnest Heaven's message, and deep cry of his heart, but would not even let him live if he kept speaking it, the wild Son of the Desert resolved to defend himself, like a man and Arab. If the Quraysh will have it so, they shall have it. Tidings, felt to be of infinite moment to them and all men, they would not listen to these; would trample them down by sheer violence, steel and murder: well, let steel try it then! Ten years more this Muhammad had; all of fighting, of breathless impetuous toil and struggle; with what result we know.

Much has been said of Muhammad's propagating his Religion by the sword. It is no doubt far nobler than what we have to boast of the Christian Religion, that it propagated itself peaceably in the way of preaching and conviction. Yet withal, if we take this for an argument of the truth or falsehood of a religion, there is a radical mistake in it. The sword indeed: but where will you get your sword! Every new opinion, at its starting, is precisely in a minority of one. In one man's head alone, there it dwells as yet. One man alone of the whole world believes it; there is one man against all men. That he takes a sword, and try to propagate with that, will do little for him. You must first get your sword! On the whole, a thing will propagate itself as it can. We do not find, of the Christian Religion either, that it always disdained the sword: I will allow a thing to struggle for itself in this world, with any sword or tongue or implement it has, or can lay hold of. We will let it preach, and pamphleteer, and fight, and to the uttermost bestir itself, and do, beak and claws, whatsoever is in it; very sure that it will, in the long run, conquer nothing which does not deserve to be conquered. What is better than itself, it cannot put away, but only what is worse. In this great Duel, Nature herself is umpire, and can do no wrong: the thing which is deepest-rooted in Nature, what we call truest, that thing and not the other will be found growing at last.

Here however, in reference to much that there is in Muhammad and his success, we are to remember what an umpire Nature is; what a greatness, composure of depth and tolerance there is in her. You take wheat to cast into the Earth's bosom: your wheat may be mixed with chaff, chopped straw, barn-sweepings, dust and all imaginable rubbish; no matter: you cast it into the kind just Earth; she grows the wheat, the whole rubbish she silently absorbs, shrouds it in, says nothing of the rubbish. The yellow wheat is growing there; the good Earth is silent about all the rest, has silently turned all the rest to some benefit too, and makes no complaint about it! So everywhere in Nature! She is true and not a lie; and yet so great, and just, and motherly in her truth. She requires of a thing only that it be genuine of heart; she will protect it if so; will not, if not so.

There is a soul of truth in all the things she ever gave harbour to. Alas, is not this the history of all highest Truth that comes or ever came into the world? The body of them all is imperfection, an element of light in darkness: to us they have to come embodied in mere Logic, in some merely scientific Theorem of the Universe; which cannot be complete; which cannot but be found, one day, incomplete, erroneous, and so die and disappear. The body of all Truth dies; and yet in all, I say, there is a soul which never dies; which in new and ever-nobler embodiment lives immortal as man himself! It is the way with Nature. The genuine essence of Truth never dies. That it be genuine, a voice from the great Deep of Nature, there is the point at Nature's judgement-seat. What we call pure or impure, is not with her the final question. Not how much chaff is in you; but whether you have any wheat. Pure? I might say to many a man: Yes, you are pure; pure enough; but you are chaff, insincere hypothesis, hearsay, formality; you never were in contact with the great heart of the Universe at all; you are properly neither pure nor impure; you are nothing, Nature has no business with you.

Muhammad's Creed we called a kind of Christianity; and really, if we look at the wild rapt earnestness with which it was believed and laid to heart, I should say a better kind than that of those miserable Syrian Sects, with their vain janglings about Homoiousion and Homoousion, the head full of worthless noise, the heart empty and dead! The truth of it is embedded in portentous error and falsehood; but the truth of it makes it be believed, not the falsehood: it succeeded by its truth. A bastard kind of Christianity, but a living kind; with a heart-life in it; not dead, chopping barren logic merely! Out of all that rubbish of Arab idolatries, argumentative theologies, traditions, subtleties, rumours and hypotheses of Greeks and Jews with their idle wiredrawings, this wild man of the Desert, with his wild sincere heart, earnest as death and life, with his great flashing natural eyesight, had seen into the kernel of the matter. Idolatry is nothing: these Wooden Idols of yours, 'ye rub them with oil and wax, and the flies stick on them,' these are wood, I tell you! They can do nothing for you; they are an impotent blasphemous pretence; a horror and abomination, if ye knew them. God alone is; God alone has power; He made us, He can kill us and keep us alive: 'Allahu akbar, God is great.' Understand that His will is the best for you; that howsoever sore to flesh-and-blood, you will find it the wisest, best: you are bound to take it so; in this world and in the next, you have no other thing that you can do!

And now if the wild idolatrous men did believe this, and with their fiery hearts lay hold of it to do it, in what form so-ever it came to them, I say it was well worthy of being believed. In one form or the other, I say it is still the one thing worthy of being believed by all men. Man does hereby become the high-priest of this Temple of a World. He is in harmony with the Decrees of the Author this World; cooperating with them, not vainly withstanding them: I know, to this day, no better definition of Duty than that same. All that is right includes itself in this of cooperating with the real Tendency of the World: you succeed by this (the World's Tendency will succeed), you are good, and in the right course there. Homoiousion, Homoousion, vain logical jangle, then or before or at any time, may jangle itself out, and go whither and how it likes: this is the thing it all struggles to mean, if it would mean anything. If it do not succeed in meaning this, it means nothing. Not that Abstractions, logical Propositions, be correctly worded or incorrectly; but that living concrete Sons of Adam do lay this to heart: that is the important point. Islam devoured all these vain jangling

Sects; and I think had right to do so. It was a Reality, direct from the great Heart of Nature once more. Arab idolatries, Syrian formulas, whatsoever was not equally real, had to go up in flame, mere dead fuel, in various senses, for this which was fire.

It was during these wild warfarings and strugglings, especially after the Flight to Makkah, that Muhammad dictated at intervals his Sacred Book, which they name Qur'an, or Reading, 'Things to be read.' This is the Work he and his disciples made so much of, asking all the world, Is not that a miracle? The Muslims regard their Qur'an with a reverence which few Christians pay even to their Bible. It is admitted everywhere as the standard of all law and all practice; the thing to be gone upon in speculation and life: the message sent direct out of Heaven, which this Earth has to conform to, and walk by; the thing to be read. Their Judges decide by it; all Muslims are bound to study it, seek in it for the light of their life. They have mosques where it is all read daily; thirty relays of priests take it up in succession, get through the whole each day. There, for twelve-hundred years, has the voice of this Book, at all moments, kept sounding through the ears and the hearts of so many men. We hear of Muslim scholars that had read it seventy-thousand times!

Very curious: if one sought for 'discrepancies of national taste,' here surely were the most eminent instance of that! We also can read the Qur'an; our Translation of it, by Sale, is known to be a very fair one. I must say, it is as toilsome reading as I ever undertook. A wearisome confused jumble, crude, incondite; endless iterations, long-windedness, entanglement; most crude, incondite; insupportable stupidity, in short! Nothing but a sense of duty could carry any European through the Qur'an. We read in it, as we might in the State-Paper Office, unreadable masses of lumber, that perhaps we may get some glimpses of a remarkable man. It is true we have it under disadvantages: the Arabs see more method in it than we. Muhammad's followers found the Qur'an lying all in fractions, as it had been written down at first promulgation; much of it, they say, on shoulder-blades of mutton, flung pellmell into a chest: and they published it, without any discoverable order as to time or otherwise;

merely trying, as would seem, and this not very strictly, to put the longest chapters first. The real beginning of it, in that way, lies almost at the end: for the earliest portions were the shortest. Read in its historical sequence it perhaps would not be so bad. Much of it, too, they say, is rhythmic; a kind of wild chanting song, in the original. This may be a great point; much perhaps has been lost in the Translation here. Yet with every allowance, one feels it difficult to see how any mortal ever could consider this Qur'an as a Book written in Heaven, too good for the Earth; as a well-written book, or indeed as a book at all; and not a bewildered rhapsody; written, so far as writing goes, as badly as almost any book ever was! So much for national discrepancies, and the standard of taste.

Yet I should say, it was not unintelligible how the Arabs might so love it. When once you get this confused coil of a Qur'an fairly off your hands, and have it behind you at a distance, the essential type of it begins to disclose itself; and in this there is a merit quite other than the literary one. If a book come from the heart, it will contrive to reach other hearts; all art and authorcraft are of small amount to that. One would say the primary character of the Qur'an is this of its genuineness, of its being a bonafide book. Prideaux, I know, and others have represented it as a mere bundle of juggleries; chapter after chapter got-up to excuse and varnish the author's successive sins, forward his ambitions and quackeries; but really it is time to dismiss all that. I do not assert

Muhammad's continual sincerity: who is continually sincere? But I confess I can make nothing of the critic, in these times, who would accuse him of deceit prepense; of conscious deceit generally, or perhaps at all; still more, of living in a mere element of conscious deceit, and writing this Qur'an as a forger and juggler would have done! Every candid eye, I think, will read the Qur'an far otherwise than so. It is the confused ferment of a great rude human soul; rude, untutored, that cannot even read, but fervent, earnest, struggling vehemently to utter itself in words. With a kind of breathless intensity he strives to utter himself; the thoughts crowd on him pellmell; for very multitude of things to say, he can get nothing said. The meaning that is in him shapes itself into no form of composition, is stated in no sequence, method, or coherence; they are not shaped at all, these thoughts of his; flung-out unshaped, as they struggle and tumble there, in their chaotic inarticulate state. We said 'stupid:' yet natural stupidity is by no means the character of Muhammad's Book; it is natural uncultivation rather. The man has not studied speaking; in the haste and pressure of continual fighting, has not time to mature himself into fit speech. The panting breathless haste and vehemence of a man struggling in the thick of battle for life and salvation; this is the mood he is in! A headlong haste; for very magnitude of meaning, he cannot get himself articulated into words. The successive utterances of a soul in that mood, coloured by the various vicissitudes of three-and-twenty years;

now well uttered, now worse: this is the Qur'an.

For we are to consider Muhammad, through these three-and-twenty years, as the centre of a world wholly in conflict. Battles with the Quraysh and Heathen, quarrels among his own people, backslidings of his own wild heart; all this kept him in a perpetual whirl, his soul knowing rest no more. In wakeful nights, as one may fancy, the wild soul of the man, tossing amid these vortices, would hail any light of a decision for them as a veritable light from Heaven; any making-up of his mind, so blessed, indispensable for him there, would seem the inspiration of a Gabriel. Forger and juggler? No, no! This great fiery heart, seething, simmering like a great furnace of thoughts, was not a juggler's. His life was a Fact for him; this God's Universe an awful Fact and Reality. He has faults enough. The man was an uncultured semi-barbarous Son of Nature, much of the Bedouin still clinging to him: we must take him for that. But for a wretched Simulacrum, a hungry Impostor without eyes or heart, practising for a mess of pottage such blasphemous swindlery, forgery of celestial documents, continual high-treason against his Maker and Self, we will not and cannot take him.

Sincerity, in all senses, seems to me the merit of the Qur'an; what had rendered it precious to the wild Arab men. It is, after all, the first and last merit in a book; gives rise to merits of all kinds, nay, at bottom, it alone can give rise to merit of any kind. Curiously, through these incondite masses of tradition, vituperation, complaint, ejaculation in the Qur'an, a vein of true direct insight, of what we might almost call poetry, is found straggling. The body of the Book is made-up of mere tradition, and as it were vehement enthusiastic extempore preaching. He returns forever to the old stories of the Prophets as they went current in the Arab memory: how Prophet after Prophet, the Prophet Abraham, the Prophet Hud, the Prophet Moses, Christian and other real and fabulous Prophets, had come to this Tribe and to that, warning men of their sin; and been received by them even as Muhammad was, which is a great solace to him. These things he repeats ten, perhaps twenty times; again and ever again, with wearisome iteration; has never done repeating them. A brave Samuel Johnson, in his forlorn garret, might con-over the Biographies of Authors in that way! This is the great staple of the Qur'an. But curiously, through all this, comes ever and anon some glance as of the real thinker and seer. He has actually an eye for the world, this Muhammad: with a certain directness and rugged vigour, he brings home still, to our heart, the thing his own heart has been opened to. I make but little of his praises of Allah, which many praise; they are borrowed I suppose mainly from the Hebrew, at least they are far surpassed there. But the eye that flashes direct into the heart of things, and sees the truth of them; this is to me a highly interesting object. Great Nature's own gift; which she bestows on all; but which only one in the thousand does not cast sorrowfully away: it is what I call sincerity of vision; the test of a sincere heart.

Muhammad can work no miracles; he often answers impatiently: I can work no miracles. I? 'I am a Public Preacher;' appointed to preach this doctrine to all creatures. Yet the world, as we can see, had really from the old been all one great miracle to him. Look over the world, says he; is it not wonderful, the work of Allah; wholly 'a sign to you,' if your eyes were open! This Earth, God made it for you; 'appointed paths in it;' you can live in it, go to and fro on it. The clouds in the dry country of Arabia, to Muhammad they are very wonderful; Great clouds, he says, born in the deep bosom of the Upper Immensity, where do they come from! They hang there, the great black monsters; pour down their rain-deluges 'to revive a dead earth,' and grass springs, and 'tall leafy palm-trees with their date-clusters hanging round. Is not that a sign?' Your cattle, too, Allah made them; serviceable dumb creatures; they change the grass into milk; you have your clothing from them, very strange creatures; they come ranking home at evening-time, 'and,' adds he, 'and are a credit to you!' Ships also, he talks often about ships: Huge moving mountains, they spread out their cloth wings, go bounding through the water there, Heaven's wind driving them; anon they lie motionless, God has withdrawn the wind, they lie dead, and cannot stir! Miracles? cries he: What miracle would you have? Are not you yourselves there? God made you, 'shaped you out of a little clay.' Ye were small once; a few years ago ye were not at all. Ye have beauty, strength, thoughts, 'ye have compassion on one another.' Old age comes on you, and gray hairs; your strength fades into feebleness; ye sink down, and again are not. 'Ye have compassion on one another;' this struck me much: Allah might have made you having no compassion on one another, how had it been then! This is a great direct thought, a glance at first-hand into the very fact of things. Rude vestiges of poetic genius, of whatsoever is best and truest, are visible in this man. A strong untutored intellect; eyesight, heart; a strong wild man, might have shaped himself into Poet, King, Priest, any kind of Hero.

To his eyes it is forever clear that this world wholly is miraculous. He sees what, as we said once before, all great thinkers, the rude Scandinavians themselves, in one way or other, have contrived to see: That this so solid-looking material world is, at bottom, in very deed, Nothing; is a visual and tactual Manifestation of God's power and presence, a shadow hung out by Him on the bosom of the void Infinite; nothing more. The mountains, he says, these great rock-mountains, they shall dissipate themselves 'like clouds;' melt into the Blue as clouds do, and not be! He figures the Earth, in the Arab fashion, Sale tells us, as an immense Plain or flat Plate of ground, the mountains are set on the top to steady it. At the Last Day they shall disappear 'like clouds;' the whole Earth shall go spinning, whirl itself off into wreck, and as dust and vapour vanish in the Inane. Allah withdraws His hand from it, and it ceases to be. The universal empire of Allah, presence everywhere of an unspeakable Power, a Splendour, and a Terror not to be named, as the true force, essence and reality, in all things whatsoever, was continually clear to this man. What a modern talks-of by the name, Forces of Nature, Laws of Nature; and does not figure as a divine thing; not even as one thing at all, but as a set of things, undivine enough, saleable, curious, good for propelling steam-ships! With our Sciences and Cyclopaedias, we are apt to forget the divineness, in those laboratories of ours. We ought not to forget it! That once well forgotten, I know not what else were worth remembering. Most sciences, I think, were then a very dead thing; withered, contentious, empty; a thistle in late autumn. The best science, without this, is but as the dead timber; it is not the growing tree and forest, which gives ever-new timber, among other things! Man cannot know either, unless he can worship in some way. His knowledge is a pedantry, and dead thistle, otherwise.

Much has been said and written about the sensuality of Muhammad's Religion; more than was just. The indulgences, criminal to us, which he permitted, were not of his appointment; he found them practised, unquestioned from immemorial times in Arabia; what he did was to curtail them, restrict them, not on one but on many sides. His Religion is not an easy one: with rigorous fasts, lavations, strict complex formulas, prayers five times a day, and abstinence from wine, it did not 'succeed by being an easy religion.' As if indeed any religion, or cause holding of religion, could succeed by that! It is a calumny on men to say that they are roused to heroic action by ease, hope of pleasure, recompense, sugar-plums of any kind, in this world or the next! In the meanest mortal there lies something nobler. The poor swearing soldier, hired to be shot, has his 'honour of a soldier,' different from drill regulations and the shilling a day. It is not to taste sweet things, but to do noble and true things, and vindicate himself under God's Heaven as a god-made Man, and that the poorest son of Adam dimly longs. Show him the way of doing that, the dullest daydrudge kindles into a hero. They wrong man greatly who say he is to be seduced by ease. Difficulty, abnegation, martyrdom, death are the allurements that act on the heart of man. Kindle the inner genial life of him, you have a flame that burns up all lower considerations. Not happiness, but something higher: one sees this even in the frivolous classes, with their 'point of honour' and the like. Not by flattering our appetites; no, by awakening the Heroic that slumbers in every heart, can any Religion gain followers.

Muhammad himself, after all that can be said about him, was not a sensual man. We shall err widely if we consider this man as a common voluptuary, intent mainly on base enjoyments, nay on enjoyments of any kind. His household was of the frugalest; his common diet barley-bread and water: sometimes for months there was not a fire once lighted on his hearth. They record with just pride that he would mend his own shoes, patch his own cloak. A poor, hard-toiling, ill-provided man; careless of what vulgar men toil for. Not a bad man, I should say; something better in him than hunger of any sort, or these wild Arab men, fighting and jostling three-and-twenty years at his hand, in close contact with him always, would not have reverenced him so! They were wild men, bursting ever and anon into quarrel, into all kinds of fierce sincerity; without right worth and manhood, no man could have commanded them. They called him Prophet, you say? Why, he stood there face to face with them; bare, not enshrined in any mystery; visibly clouting his own cloak, cobbling his own shoes; fighting, counselling, ordering in the midst of them: they must have seen what kind of a man he was, let him be called what you like! No emperor with his tiaras was obeyed as this man in a cloak of his own clouting. During three-and-twenty years of rough trial. I find something of a veritable Hero necessary for that, of itself.

His last words are a prayer; broken ejaculations of a heart struggling up, in trembling hope, towards its Maker. We cannot say that his religion made him worse; it made him better; good, not bad. Generous things are recorded of him: when he lost his Daughter, the thing he answers is, in his own dialect, everyway sincere, and yet equivalent to that of Christians, 'The Lord giveth, and the Lord taketh away; blessed be the name of the Lord.' He answered in like manner of Za'id, his emancipated well-beloved

Slave, the second of the believers, Za'id had fallen in the War of Tabuk, the first of Muhammad's fightings with the Greeks. Muhammad said, It was well; Za'id had done his Master's work, Sa'id had now gone to his Master: it was all well with Za'id. Yet Za'id's daughter found him weeping over the body; the old gray-haired man melting in tears! "What do I see?" said she, "You see a friend weeping over his friend." He went out for the last time into the mosque, two days before his death; asked, If he injured any man? Let his own back bear the stripes. If he owed any man? A voice answered, "Yes, me three dirhams," borrowed on such an occasion. Muhammad ordered them to be paid: "Better be in shame now," said he, "than at the Day of Judgement." You remember

Khadijah, and the "No, by Allah!" Traits of that kind show us the genuine man, the brother of us all, brought through twelve centuries, the veritable Son of our common Mother.

Withal I like Muhammad for his total freedom from cant. He is a rough self-helping son of the wilderness; does not pretend to be what he is not. There is no ostentatious pride in him; but neither does he go much upon humility: he is there as he can be, in cloak and shoes of his own clouting; speaks plainly to all manner of Persian Kings, Greek Emperors, what it is they are bound to do; knows well enough, about himself, 'the respect due unto you.' In a life-and-death war with Bedouins, cruel things could not fail; but neither are acts of mercy, of noble natural pity and generosity wanting. Muhammad makes no apology for the one, nor boast of the other. They were each the free dictate of his heart; each called for, there and then. Not a mealy-mouthed man! A candid ferocity, if the case call for it, is in him; he does not mince matters! The War of Tabuk is a thing he often speaks of: his men refused, many of them, to march on that occasion; pleaded the heat of the weather, the harvest, and so forth; he can never forget that. Your harvest? It lasts for a day. What will become of your harvest through all Eternity? Hot weather? Yes, it was hot; 'but Hell will be hotter!' Sometimes a rough sarcasm turns-up: He says to the unbelievers, Ye shall have the just measure of your deeds at the Great Day. They will be weighed out to you; ye shall not have short weight!

Everywhere he fixes the matter in his eye; he sees it: his heart, now and then, is as if struck dumb by the greatness of it. 'Assuredly,' he says: that word, in the Qur'an, is written-down sometimes as a sentence by itself: 'Assuredly.'

No Dilettantism in this Muhammad; it is a business of Reprobation and Salvation with him, of Time and Eternity: he is in deadly earnest about it! Dilettantism, hypothesis, speculation, a kind of amateur search for Truth, toying and coquetting with Truth: this is the sorest sin. The root of all other imaginable sins. It consists in the heart and soul of the man never having been open to Truth; 'living in a vain show. Such a man not only utters and produces falsehoods, but is himself a falsehood. The rational moral principle, spark of the Divinity, is sunk deep in him, in quiet paralysis of life-death. The very falsehoods of Muhammad are truer than the truths of such a man. He is the insincere man: smooth-polished, respectable in some times and places; inoffensive, says nothing harsh to anybody; most cleanly, just as carbonic acid is, which is death and poison.

We will not praise Muhammad's moral precepts as always of the superfinest sort; yet it can be said that there is always a tendency to good in them; that they are the true dictates of a heart aiming towards what is just and true. The sublime forgiveness of Christianity, turning of the other cheek when the one has been smitten, is not here: you are to revenge yourself, but it is to be in measure, not overmuch, or beyond justice. On the other hand, Islam, like any great Faith, and insight into the essence of man, is a perfect equaliser of men: the soul of one believer outweighs all earthly kingships; all men, according to Islam too, are equal. Muhammad insists not on the propriety of giving alms, but on the necessity of it: he marks down by law how much you are to give, and it is at your peril if you neglect. The tenth part of a man's annual income, whatever that may be, is the property of the poor, of those that are afflicted and need help. Good all this: the natural voice of humanity, of pity and equity dwelling in the heart of this wild Son of Nature speaks so.

Muhammad's Paradise is sensual, his Hell sensual: true; in the one and the other there is enough that shocks all spiritual feeling in us. But we are to recollect that the Arabs already had it so; that Muhammad, in whatever he changed of it, softened and diminished all this. The worst sensualities, too, are the work of doctors, followers of his, not his work. In the Qur'an there is really very little said about the joys of Paradise; they are intimated rather than insisted on. Nor is it forgotten that the highest joys even there shall be spiritual; the pure Presence of the Highest, this shall infinitely transcend all other joys. He says, 'Your salutation shall be, Peace.' Salam, Have Peace!—the thing that all rational souls long for, and seek, vainly here below, as the one blessing. 'Ye shall sit on seats, facing one another: all grudges shall be taken away out of your hearts.' All grudges! Ye shall love one another freely;

for each of you, in the eyes of his brothers, there will be Heaven enough!

In reference to this of the sensual Paradise and Muhammad's sensuality, the sorest chapter of all for us, there were many things to be said; which it is not convenient to enter upon here. Two remarks only I shall make, and therewith leave it to your candour. The first is furnished me by Goethe; it is a casual hint of his which seems well worth taking note of. In one of his Delineations, the Meister's Travels it is, the hero comes upon a Society of men with very strange ways, one of which was this: "We require," says the Master, "that each of our people shall restrict himself in one direction," shall go right against his desire in one matter, and make himself do the thing he does not wish, "should we allow him the greater latitude on all other sides." There seems to me a great justness in this. Enjoying things which are pleasant; that is not the evil: it is the reducing of our moral self to slavery by them that is. Let a man assert withal that he is king over his habitudes; that he could and would shake them off, on cause shown: this is an excellent law. The Month Ramadan for the Muslim, much in Muhammad's Religion, much in his own Life, bears in that direction; if not by forethought, or clear purpose of moral improvement on his part, then by a certain healthy manful instinct, which is as good.

But there is another thing to be said about the Muslim Heaven and Hell. This namely, that, however gross and material they may be, they are an emblem of an everlasting truth, not always so well remembered elsewhere. That gross sensual Paradise of his; that horrible flaming Hell; the great enormous Day of Judgement he perpetually insists on: what is all this but a rude shadow, in the rude Bedouin imagination, of that grand spiritual Fact, and Beginning of Facts, which it is ill for us too if we do not all know and feel: the Infinite Nature of Duty? That man's actions here are of infinite moment to him, and never die or end at all; that man, with his little life, reaches upwards high as Heaven, downwards low as Hell, and in his threescore years of Time holds an Eternity fearfully and wonderfully hidden: all this had burnt itself, as in flame-characters, into the wild Arab soul. As in flame and lightning, it stands written there; awful, unspeakable, ever present to him. With bursting earnestness, with a fierce savage sincerity, halt, articulating, not able to articulate, he strives to speak it, bodies it forth in that Heaven and that Hell. Bodied forth in what way you will, it is the first of all truths. It is venerable under all embodiments. What is the chief end of man here below? Muhammad has answered this question, in a way that might put some of us to shame! He does not, like a Bentham, a Paley, take Right and Wrong, and calculate the profit and loss, ultimate pleasure of the one and of the other; and summing all up by addition and subtraction into a net result, ask you, Whether on the whole the Right does not preponderate considerably? No; it is not better to do the one than the other; the one is to the other as life is to death, as

Heaven is to Hell. The one must in nowise be done, the other in nowise left undone. You shall not measure them; they are incommensurable: the one is death eternal to a man, the other is life eternal. Benthamic Utility, virtue by Profit and Loss; reducing this God's world to a dead brute Steam-engine, the infinite celestial Soul of Man to a kind of Hay-balance for weighing hay and thistles on, pleasures and pains on. If you ask me which gives, Muhammad or they, the beggarlier and falser view of Man and his Destinies in this Universe, I will answer, It is not Muhammad!

On the whole, we will repeat that this Religion of Muhammad's is a kind of Christianity; has a genuine element of what is spiritually highest looking through it, not to be hidden by all its imperfections. The Scandinavian God Wish, the god of all rude men, this has been enlarged into a Heaven by Muhammad; but a Heaven symbolical of sacred Duty, and to be earned by faith and welldoing, by valiant action, and a divine patience which is still more valiant. It is Scandinavian Paganism, and a truly celestial element superadded to that. Call it not false; look not at the falsehood of it, look at the truth of it. For these twelve centuries, it has been the religion and life-guidance of the fifth part of the whole kindred of Mankind. Above all things, it has been a religion heartily believed. These Arabs believe their religion, and try to live by it! No Christians, since the early ages, or only perhaps the English Puritans in modern times, have ever stood by their Faith as the Muslim do by theirs, believing it wholly, fronting Time with it, and Eternity with it. This night the watchman on the streets of Cairo when he cries, "Who goes?" will hear from the passenger, along with his answer, "There is no deity save Allah." Allahu akbar, Islam, sounds through the souls, and whole daily existence, of these dusky millions. Zealous missionaries preach it abroad among Malays, black Papuans, brutal Idolators; displacing what is worse, nothing that is better or good.

To the Arab Nation it was a birth from darkness into light; Arabia first came alive by means of it. A poor shepherd people, roaming unnoticed in its deserts since the creation of the world: a Hero-Prophet was sent down to them with a word they could believe: see, the unnoticed becomes world-notable, the small has grown world-great; within one century afterwards, Arabia is at Granada on this hand, at Delhi on that; glancing in valour and splendour and the light of genius, Arabia shines through long ages over a great section of the world. Belief is great, live-giving. The history of a Nation becomes fruitful, soul-elevating, great, so soon as it believes. These Arabs, the man Muhammad, and that one century, it is not as if a spark had fallen, one spark, on a world of what seemed black unnoticeable sand; but lo, the sand proves explosive powder, blazes heaven-high from Delhi to Granada! I said, the Great Man was always as lightning out of Heaven; the rest of men waited for him like fuel, and then they too would flame.

Goodword English Publications

Simple Wisdom (HB), Maulana Wahiduddin Khan

Simple Wisdom (PB), Maulana Wahiduddin Khan

The True Jihad, Maulana Wahiduddin Khan

Tabligh Movement, Maulana Wahiduddin Khan

A Treasury of the Quran, Maulana Wahiduddin Khan

Woman Between Islam and Western Society,
Maulana Wahiduddin Khan

Woman in Islamic Shari'ah, Maulana Wahiduddin Khan

The Ideology of Peace, Maulana Wahiduddin Khan

Indian Muslims, Maulana Wahiduddin Khan

Introducing Islam, Maulana Wahiduddin Khan

Islam: Creator of the Modern Age, Maulana Wahiduddin Khan

Islam: The Voice of Human Nature,
Maulana Wahiduddin Khan

Islam Rediscovered, Maulana Wahiduddin Khan

Words of the Prophet Muhammad,
Maulana Wahiduddin Khan

God Arises, Maulana Wahiduddin Khan

The Call of the Qur'an, Maulana Wahiduddin Khan

Building a Strong and Prosperous India and Role of Muslims,
Maulana Wahiduddin Khan

Islam As It Is, Maulana Wahiduddin Khan

Sermons of the Prophet Muhammad, Assad Nimer Busool

Bouquet of the Noble Hadith, Assad Nimer Busool

Forty Hadith, Assad Nimer Busool

Hijrah in Islam, Dr. Zafarul Islam Khan

Palestine Documents, Dr. Zafarul Islam Khan

At the Threshold of New Millennium, Dr. Zafarul Islam Khan

Islamic Sciences, Waqar Husaini

Islamic Thought..., Waqar Husaini

The Qur'an for Astronomy, Waqar Husaini

A Dictionary of Muslim Names, Prof. S.A. Rahman

Let's Speak Arabic, Prof. S.A. Rahman

Teach Yourself Arabic, Prof. S.A. Rahman

Islamic Medicine, Edward G. Browne

Literary History of Persia (Vol.1 & 2), Edward G. Browne

Literary History of Persia (Vol.3 & 4), Edward G. Browne

The Soul of the Quran, Saniyasnain Khan

Presenting the Quran, Saniyasnain Khan

The Wonderful Universe of Allah, Saniyasnain Khan

A-Z Ready Reference of the Quran (Based on the Translation by Abdullah Yusuf Ali), Mohammad Imran Erfani

The Alhambra, Washington Irving

The Encyclopaedic Index of the Quran, Dr. Syed Muhammad Osama

The Essentials of Islam, Al-Haj Saeed Bin Ahmed Al Lootah

Glossary of the Quran, Aurang Zeb Azmi

Introducing Arabic, Michael Mumisa

Arabic-English Dictionary, J.G. Hava

The Arabs in History, Prof. Bernard Lewis

A Basic Reader for the Holy Quran, Syed Mahmood Hasan

The Beauty of Makkah and Madinah, Mohamed Amin

A Brief Illustrated Guide to Understanding Islam, I.A. Ibrahim

The Concept of Society in Islam and Prayers in Islam, Dr. Syed Abdul Latif

Decisive Moments in the History of Islam, Muhammad Abdullah Enan

The Handy Concordance of the Quran, Aurang Zeb Azmi

The Hadith for Beginners, Dr. Muhammad Zubayr Siddiqui

A Handbook of Muslim Belief, Dr. Ahmad A Galwash

Heart of the Koran, Lex Hixon

A History of Arabian Music, Henry George Farmer

A History of Arabic Literature, Clément Huart

How Greek Science Passed to Arabs, De Lacy O' Leary

Humayun Nama, Gulbadan Bano

Islam and the Divine Comedy, Miguel Asin

Islam and Ahmadism, Muhammad Iqbal